FOYER PLEASURE

The Golden Age of Cinema Lobby Cards

FOYER PLEASURE

The Golden Age of Cinema Lobby Cards

John Kobal & V. A. Wilson

A *Delilah* BOOK
DISTRIBUTED BY THE PUTNAM PUBLISHING GROUP
N E W • Y O R K

ACKNOWLEDGEMENTS

Information for the introduction to this book was excessively hard to come by since almost nothing has been written on the subject of lobby cards, except for passing references in David Chierichetti's fine introduction to *The Movie Poster Book* (Dutton, 1979), and David Robinson's introduction to *50 Years of Movie Posters* (Hamlyn, 1973). I am therefore deeply indebted to the author and film historian David DelValle, who came up with information that has proved invaluable.

I should like also to acknowledge my gratitude to Bill Douglas and Richard Tanner, who listened to and advised on the captions for the individual lobby cards, and the gentleman in the row behind me on the plane, who, on spotting me trying to work surrounded by some of these items, interrupted out of curiosity and stayed to lighten the journey with his useful hints.

JOHN KOBAL

PUBLISHER'S NOTE

Great care has been taken in the reproduction of the lobby cards in this book, but there were occasional blemishes on the original material which could not be removed.

A Delilah Book
Delilah Communications, Ltd.
118 East 25 Street
New York, N.Y. 10010

ISBN: 0-933328-76-1
Library of Congress Catalog Card Number: 83-45222

First published in the United States of America
by Delilah Communications, Ltd. in 1983.
Originally published in Great Britain
by Aurum Press Limited in 1982.

Colour separations by Latent Image
Phototypeset by Bookworm Typesetting, Manchester
Typographic design by Neil H. Clitheroe

FOREWORD   Benny Green

In the years of my childhood, every Sunday afternoon, winter or summer, rain or shine, preconceived as any calendar, my mother, her sister my maiden aunt, and myself would go and stand in the queue outside one of our three local cinemas, the Paramount, the Dominion and the Astoria. To say that we were going to the pictures would be an over-simplification. We were performing a most intricate and intimate tribal dance, fulfilling the one non-utilitarian event in our diaries, voicing the only aesthetic judgment available to us, paying tribute to the one mythology which had any real relevance to our lives. The movies were the nearest thing to a world religion. But it was a pagan religion, a religion on the lines of Olympus, only instead of Zeus and Hera we had Gable and Harlow, instead of Daphnis and Chloë Fred and Ginger, instead of the nine Muses the Three Stooges. And it all worked in exactly the same way. The gods and goddesses up there on the screen were at once intimately familiar and thrillingly removed from us. We could anticipate their every move and yet never remotely aspire to meeting any of them. The production companies were selling a dream, a world that was two-dimensional only, for which reason they had to strive to condition us so that by the time we entered the cathedral we were in a suitably receptive, that is to say non-critical, frame of mind.

But although our critical faculties were numbed – by the chief commissionaire so proudly accoutred in the regalia of a Montenegran Vice-Admiral, by the grandeur of the foyer, the livery of the usherettes, the thickness of the carpets, the softness of the lighting – we were still not quite rendered unconscious. One day, in considering these cinemas of my formative years, it occurred to me that there was something very odd about their construction. Architecturally speaking, they went in like a lion and came out like a lamb. They were all grandiloquence at the front, all squalor at the back. These picture palaces were fabulous monsters, the jabberwocks and bandersnatches of modern design, incredible beasts with enormous leonine heads, hollow bodies and no tails to speak of at all, optimistic arrangements in bricks and mortar, steel and stucco, knocked up in the hope that the Byzantine splendour of their entrances might distract from the back alleys of their exits.

The hope was not only justified but understandable. The customer needed to be browbeaten into acquiescence of the dubious splendours to come, hence the imposing foyers. But once you had his money you could bundle him out without due ceremony through the back alleys. The devices thought up to deck out those foyers were sometimes remarkable. I remember that the Empire, Leicester Square, actually had a large fishpond near the box office, in which live goldfish disported in the leaden air. And although the Empire was exceptional in this regard, it was like every other cinema in Britain in the approach it adopted to filling its foyer walls. In order to massage the customer gently as he proceeded on his journey from the street to the dream-world the management hung photographic portraits of the gods and goddesses, or scenes from the thrilling sagas to come. It was a sort of prelude to the service proper, a respectful promenade flanked by the deities of the studio system. How ironic that all these years after, while all recollection of the movies has gone, the look and style of those pictures on the walls remain.

At the Paramount Dorothy Lamour hung languid and wet-lipped, gazing at some focus of her romantic reverie just right of the camera. At the Dominion Gable looked dashing with his pencil-moustache and a polka-dotted tie. At the Astoria James Stewart gazed dolefully into the eyes of Jean Arthur. Some of the stars photographed better than they acted. Harlow was an example, and the cynics said that Mae West was another. As for the scenes of action, which we took for a managerial afterthought but which had really been the result of much discussion, some money and a little artistic enterprise, they burned their images into our minds until it became impossible for us not to buy a ticket and find out what happened. I recall a still from *Gunga Din*, with the warriors of the British Raj perched high on a papier-maché hill mouthing defiance at Mohammed Khan or whoever.

And Holmes, complete with deerstalker and magnifying glass, apparently examining the texture of the tweed of Watson's overcoat. I can vaguely call up Cap'n Andy in *Show Boat* leaning over the rail of the S.S. *Cotton Blossom* with a smile that the plot of the picture would soon have wiped off his face. And a wide-eyed Groucho Marx brandishing a cigar in the face of Margaret Dumond while in the background Harpo, in jockey-cap, ogled Chico. There was one of the dashing William Powell in a smart trilby, accompanied by Mrs Nick Charles (Myrna Loy) and a small terrier (Asta) intent on getting in the way of the script of *The Thin Man*. There was Grable in a grass skirt, Garbo with a page-boy hairdo, Dick Powell in a milk-white suit sharing a large chair with Joan Blondell in a milk-white dress.

Across these portraits was printed in bold letters the name of the film, plus something modestly superlative like 'Thrill to the greatest love story ever told', or 'Watch this thriller if you dare', or 'The happiest, smilingest, singingest little picture you will ever remember'. Sometimes disenchantment struck, when we realised that the action stills did not always appear in the production they advertised. From this we deduced that the pictures on the wall were an entity in themselves, that they were being manufactured for the express purpose of beguiling us. Far from being angry or feeling put-upon, we exulted in the subtleties of the whole game, and aspired to ownership of one or more of the portraits. Alas, none of us ever succeeded. Not even the most felonious among us ever figured out a way of detaching the mooning Miss Lamour or the vibrant Rita Hayworth from their cinematic moorings. We used to wonder what happened to them all in the end. Did the cinema manager just chuck them away? Or send them back to California? Or sell them off to the highest bidder? Whatever the answer, it seems that more than enough of the murals of the great days of the movies have survived to gratify the heart of a once-dedicated votary. This delectable volume lures us once more into the jaws of the vanished picture palace, with its promise of pleasures to come.

INTRODUCTION

The Lobby Card – garish, lively, electric, vulgar, often silly –
was a form of advertising that revolutionized the look of
graphics. Lobby Cards were sent out by the publicity
departments of the Hollywood studios in sets of eight to
twenty images reflecting the content of a newly released
movie. Their purpose: to lure the movie-going public into
theatres across the country.

Their use in the promotion of films dates from the earliest
years of moviemaking, after the trusts had been broken and
the triumphant independents (later to become the Majors –
Universal, Paramount, Metro, Fox) had won their victory
by creating the Star System. It became clear to producers that
they could not ignore the public's desire for their favorite
movie stars and so the studios hired publicity men to trumpet
the glories of these 'individual players'. Writers and pro-
moters were hired, men and women who came from the
muckraking fields of journalism, from Wild West traveling
shows, from fairgrounds and from circuses across the
country. The press reacted with glee to every bit of news
connected with stars and moviemakers (the fact that most of
it consisted of invented stories didn't seem to matter; after all,
it fueled ambitions and hopes, and that sold newspapers).
From this came the pressbook, an illustrated trade publica-
tion that accompanied each film as it was sent to newspapers
and exhibitors. The pressbook contained ads, plot summar-
ies, and suggestions of how best to exploit the moving
pictures they were showing (the first pressbook was twelve
pages long; in later years they were as long as one hundred
pages and were the size of a table top). Newspapers helped to
sell the stars and the stars helped to sell newspapers. Film
posters, large, lush, colorful, bold – initially modeled on

circus posters and theatrical productions, as well as book jackets – were created. They quickly acquired a look all their own, a style that was actually much more daring and ingenious than the advertising poster of that time.

These cards – 11″ × 14″ eye catchers found in the foyers of movie houses – were, along with bubble-gum, hamburgers, seamless nylons and the Joan Crawford 'fuck me' pumps, a uniquely American creation. They were a direct offshoot of the Circus Posters that were plastered across barn doors and backwood fences and promised a world of wonders when the circus came to town, luring many a Toby Tyler to run away from home and join a magic world.

The earliest known Lobby Cards, dating back to 1908, were part of a weighty bundle of advertising material provided by the early film companies to theatre owners with their two-reelers. These cards – sepia or duo-tinted, 8″×10″ in size – were mounted on easels beside the box office window or inside the lobby. They were little more than murky reproductions of stills, the result of a brown and white rotogravure process that lacked any clear-cut whites and browns. Unlike the stills, the images were selected to give a sense of the story line of the movie and to supply the credits. The rotogravure process used in printing the Lobby Cards made them more durable than the fragile photographic stock on which movie stills were printed. Even then, some of the cards would have faint coloring applied by hand or by stencil; these give little indication of the splendors to come only a few years later.

As movie-making and movie-selling became more sophisticated (even before sound), Lobby Cards became more lavish, imaginative and dimensional, using kinetic designs that surrounded images; often these border designs were more interesting than the photographs they decorated. A typical set of cards promoted ROMANCE! DRAMA! TERROR! LAUGHTER! TEARS! ('Hurry, hurry, hurry – see lovely Mary Pickford in the arms of her boyfriend, Jock! See her cry! See her tortured by the Huns!')

By 1914 de Mille had made the first feature length movie filmed in California, *The Squawman*; Griffith was starting on his epic *Birth of a Nation*; Keystone comedies were achieving world-wide popularity with two-reelers starring Charles Chaplin and Mabel Normand; serial thrillers like *The Perils of Pauline* were the rage of the nation. Now Lobby Cards became more elaborate, reflecting the extravagant pace or mood of the movie they advertised. *Ben Hur* (MGM 1926) is an example. Directed by Fred Niblo and starring Ramon Navarro, a pretty Mexican boy created to rival Valentino as one of the great lovers of the silent screen, *Ben Hur* was one of the most expensive silent films made up to that time. It was begun in Metro's Hollywood studios, but was filmed primarily on location in impoverished post-war Italy. Its success on its initial release was colossal and five years later, in 1931, MGM reissued it with a soundtrack to reach new audiences. (Note headline at top left of title card.) Portrayed here is the film's spectacular center piece, the chariot race at Antioch between the two childhood friends turned mortal enemies – Ben Hur (Ramon Navarro) and his team of whites, and Messala (Francis X. Bushman) and his team of blacks. Although this is the title card of the set, note that only the name of the film appears here; by the time of the film's reissue Navarro was on the wane and Bushman was completely forgotten.

The cards grew to 11″×14″ (this became the standard size) and were offered in sets of no less than eight exciting scenes for the average film, and as many as sixteen for the new super productions.

As printing techniques evolved, so did the flair and imagination with which these cards were designed. Film historian David Chierichetti has described the process thus:

'In the early 1920s Paramount developed a new and distinctive style for its cards. Printing on very white stock and using an offset image with dense blacks and sharply detailed halftones, Paramount's publicity department cut out the figures of stars [as with Gloria Swanson in *Zaza*, see page 27] and surrounded them with completely non-realistic highly stylized drawn sets rendered in the most brilliant possible colors.'[1]

During this time the selection of the images, the imaginative artwork bordering the images, the creatively hand-tinted subjects and the brilliant colors, combined to create a piece of artwork that conveyed the mood of the film more eloquently than the images selected for use. While it might seem ironic that these Lobby Cards were produced in blazing colors for what were after all, with a few rare exceptions, black and white films, the point of the posters and Lobby Cards was to convey the excitement of the product they were selling. When a silent film did include spectacular tinted sequences or, as with Fairbanks' *The Black Pirate* (see page 31), was shot in one of the early color processes, the Lobby Cards would provide this information by pointing it out in the logo. Confusion only arose much later, when color became an established part of movies. But Lobby Cards for all films – whether color or black and white – were produced in full color. Here is a colored photograph taken by Alex Kahle during the filming of *Stagecoach* (UA 1939) on location at Monument Valley. The photograph has been hand-tinted, despite the fact that the film itself is in black and white. Someone in the art department felt a striking way to draw attention to a new kind of western was to create the illusion

[1] *The Movie Poster Book*, Steve Schapiro and David Chierichetti (Dutton, 1979)

of looking through a telescope. This particular image has become one of the most recognizable images of all movies. Note, there are no names of stars featured on this Lobby Card. Ford was selling the glory and scope of the west.

The Lobby Card in blazing colors (many, like Fairbanks' magnificent *Thief of Baghdad*, employing gold and silver tints in their lettering, created the illusion of Persian miniatures), became an exciting amalgamation of poster art and photograph, with the borders following the same fanciful artwork that was used for the even more elaborate and stylish

DOUGLAS FAIRBANKS
IN *The* THIEF OF BAGDAD

one-sheet posters. What made this possible was the emergence of the photogelatin or heliotype process. David Chierichetti writes, '. . . it used a metal plate covered with photosensitized gelatin that was exposed to light through a regular photograph negative. The gelatin hardened in varying degrees according to the amount of light received, the darkest parts of the image turned hardest. Photogelatin printing was best suited to the smaller cards because it was almost as fine-textured as a photograph, lacking the grains or dots of lithography. The cards were meant to be viewed closely and usually contained much more written material than the posters.'[2]

The publicity departments would pick eight to ten strong images from the movie to attract attention. Here, for *Captain Marvel*, a 1941 serial based on the comic strip, an ordinary mortal named Billy has just been given the power by Zeus (far right) to fight crime and corruption in the world. 'Just say the word Shazam (S for the wisdom of Solomon . . . H for the power of Hercules . . . A for the strength of Atlas . . . Z for the thunder bolt of Zeus . . . A for the justice of Athena . . . M for the speed of Mercury) . . . and with your last breath you will be transformed into an imitation Superman.'

As well as the logo of the distribution company, the film's title, the name of the star, plot outlines and lines of dialogue from the film, highly visible when used out of context, would also be part of the integrated design. A classic example is one of the cards for *Babes in Arms* (MGM 1940). There is a word for design like this, 'Schmerm'. Advertising designers who worked with luxury accounts like Camel or Lux or Studebaker looked down on Hollywood advertising designers. They failed to recognize the almost impossible conditions of the Hollywood Ad. departments in selling a film. The poster designs and title cards would have endless

[2] *The Movie Poster Book*

contractual commitments. The design had to reveal something of the film; it had to give the names of the stars while paying attention to the size of the names. (It might say in Judy Garland's contract that her name had to be above the title, and also had to be the same size as her co-star. A year later her name would be as big as the title and two years after that bigger, until finally there was no title, just JUDY.) Then it had to be stated that the movie was a musical. The card had to have a photograph from the movie, plus a cartoon, plus the names of the supporting players who must have had better agents than either the director, the composer or the producer of the film. (See *I'm No Angel,* page 84; *Dark Victory*, page 135; *Queen Christina*, page 87.)

While the title (or main) card in each set was often identical to the 22″×28″ one sheet, and in some cases was one and the same, the men employed to select for the lobbies the eight or so images out of the hundreds of stills taken, as well as doing the specially composed art, were creating ever more fanciful artwork and evocative montage effects. These could be used in combination on one card with several shots of the star, or various scenes from the film. (See page 65, *Werewolf of London.*)

Executive or star approval was required at each stage of the lettering and design. The memo from the main office to the boys in publicity usually requested only that the selected stills run in succession with the plot, but the actual choice of images was left to whatever underling was available; this accounts for some bizarre selections which sometimes excluded images of the featured player – or played up supporting actors in the film. Of course the great stars, Swanson, Chaplin, Pickford, Crawford, Fairbanks and the legendary bee-stung lipped Mae Murray, who were actively employed in the production of their own films, made sure

" 'President' Rooney and his First Lady, Judy arrive at the 'White House' ! "

that they saw all the material about them before the finished artwork was sent out to the poster company where the color separations were made. Their co-stars had no such luck.

The New York based poster companies who specialized in printing studio advertising material had their own staff of artists who designed for many of the smaller studios, among them Republic and Monogram. Very often the men who selected the images for these films either hadn't seen them or couldn't have cared less.

Often a set for one of the Republic features consisted only of dust-raising long shots in which the stars were distant images, or, conversely, might contain nothing but unexciting close-ups of two or three of the featured players posed for the poster art and giving no clue to the story in which they featured. (See *Thunderbolt*.)

By the early forties the Lobbies were less exciting. They were badly reproduced, weakly colored scene stills from the films, printed on inexpensive paper stock (due in part to the wartime paper shortage, and to a general decline in interest by those in charge).

Throughout the years studios employed famous American artists to design their advertising; the forties saw such popular American artists and illustrators as Norman Rockwell (*Magnificent Ambersons, Song of Bernadette, The Razor's Edge*), Dan Sayre Groesbeck (*Northwest Mounted Police, The Buccaneer*), masters of the pin-up like Vargas (*Moon Over Miami, The Flame of New Orleans, Ziegfeld Follies*), George Petty (*The Petty Girl*) and others, employed on occasions to design the posters that would subsequently be adapted for Lobby Cards. Thus, Vargas' drawing of a languorously indolent peek-a-booish blonde Dietrich for *The Flame of New Orleans* (U 1941), decorated the borders of the Lobbies. The seventies and eighties have seen a resurgence in the use of famous artists to design movie posters: Frank Frazetta (*The Gauntlet, Conan, The Barbarian*), Richard Amsel (*Chinatown, The Sting, Raiders of the Lost Ark*), Peter Max (*The Yellow Submarine, Joanna*) and their designs have also found their way to Lobby Cards.

But the real hard sell was not with the use of a famous illustrator but using an element of the film as a gimmick or a tease. This was frequently used for horror films. For Lon Chaney's *Phantom of the Opera* (U 1925) or Karloff's *The Old Dark House* (U 1932), starring these masters of make-up, it became part of the advertising gimmick to have their make-up remain a mystery, and faces were blotted out. When horrifying features had been revealed and the films were reissued, their faces were reinstated on the Lobby Cards.

As movies progressed from silent to sound, so did the Lobby Card. While publicity departments were momentarily baffled by the advent of sound – a picture can be hand painted but how to make it talk? – gimmicks were dreamt up in an attempt to solve that problem. With the arrival of *The Jazz Singer*, sound became the novelty that had to be sold. In the foyers of movie theatres, Lobby Cards were combined with the newly invented Talkie Card, a short lived forerunner of today's home video cassettes. Stills from the film showed the cast in static poses, as a result of being grouped round invisible microphones, quoting lines of dialogue from the movie. They were placed on a revolving drum linked to a recording of snippets of dialogue that would go on as each card popped up.

When the use of color came along as the next box office gimmick, the imaginative hand-tinted black and white images were replaced by color stills, though the reproduction was often far more artificial and less effective than before.

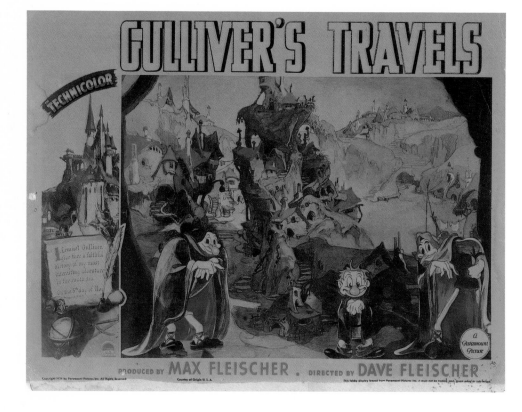

But there were exceptions, such as the Lobby Cards for *Duel in the Sun* (UA 1946), the first *A Star Is Born* (UA 1937), Disney's *Snow White and the Seven Dwarfs* (see page 126), *Fantasia* and the Fleischers' *Gulliver's Travels* (PAR. 1939), which could not have failed to interest budding commercial art students. *Gulliver's Travels* came about because of the overwhelming success of Disney's *Snow White*, his first feature-length animated film, released a year before. Only the Fleischers (Max and Dave), creators of Popeye and Betty Boop, were able to make successfully another feature length animated film. Perhaps one of the reasons for the film's success was the background, directly based on the work of the great children's book illustrator Arthur Rackham. The image here is a cell from the film; these colors, though somewhat faded, approximate to the color of the film. (Note the technicolor banner.) When the studios began to employ Cinemascope, Vista Vision, 3D and Smell-O-Vision, Lobby Cards, along with the rest of the industry, had had it.

As the design of Lobby Cards started to decline, the spell they had exerted for all those years began to have another unforeseen effect. A handful of ardent movie fans began to collect them. Since there was no simple way of obtaining these cards, fans employed the 'Truffaut Method' – now you see the Lobby Card in the foyer now you don't, as a happy buttoned-up fan steals off into the night. This early form of collecting was romanticized in French fan-turned-director François Truffaut's *Day For Night*.

Collecting did not come properly into its own until the 60s, when Hollywood's past became the obsession of the present, first as camp, then as nostalgia, finally as art – and investment. Only recently has the name of the illustrating artist had much importance for the collector; the star was all. Now these items – whose value had initially been less than the cost of printing because of the enormous quantities in which they were produced – have reached astronomical prices. In 1964 a Lobby Card for a film like *Captain Blood* starring Errol Flynn, or *Casablanca*, could be purchased for $5 or less. (As a matter of interest, I first came across Lobby Cards in the basement of the British Film Institute in London where they were lying around in huge bundles to be given away.) By 1970, their price had begun its upward spiral. A *Captain Blood* title card today is worth around $650. *Casablanca*'s title card (see page 138) would fetch $1000. (The scene cards, depending on Bogart being in them, are around $400 a card. Without Bogart, you can get one for $50.) The title card for the 1935 horror classic *The Bride of Frankenstein* has changed hands for $3500, the scenes go for a minimum of $1500. Similar prices apply to such classics as *King Kong, The Wizard of Oz*, films starring Garbo (see pages 34, 87) and Dietrich (pages 71, 79, 107); the films Dietrich made with Josef von Sternberg are among the most valuable of all. Since the salacious allegations about him, any advertising material with Errol Flynn on it has increased in value. These prices apply predominantly to 1930s films, but also include silent films starring Rudolph Valentino (see page 37), Mary Pickford (see page 25), Fairbanks and Charles Chaplin, and classics like *Ben Hur* (see page 11), and any films by directors like Griffith and von Stroheim. As these items became increasingly scarce, a new crop of legends appeared such as the classics of 1940 film noir – *This Gun For Hire, The Maltese Falcon, The Glass Key* – and of course the great Disney animation features (see page 126). All of these Lobby Cards are now valued at prices comparable to those of movie posters. To many dealers, Lobby Cards are even preferable items for the same reason that they appealed initially, their size – 11″×14″ is preferred. An entire set of eight Lobby

Slowly recognition came to him... the girl he had bitten... was the same girl who had befriended him as a puppy.

LASSIE
COURAGE
of LASSIE
in Technicolor
ELIZABETH TAYLOR
FRANK MORGAN·TOM DRAKE

ANN SHERIDAN ROBERT CUMMINGS RONALD REAGAN BETTY FIELD

KINGS ROW

Presented by WARNER BROS. Pictures Inc.

Cards for *King Kong* recently sold in LA for $8000, while at a 1981 auction held by Phillips in New York a new high was reached when a set of cards for *Dracula* (U 1931) went for nearly $9000.

While these are rare and exceptionally fine in design, other items have vacillated dramatically in price. A good example are those advertising materials for any movies with Ronald Reagan. With the exception of *King's Row*, his only memorable movie, Reagan was never worthy of attention as a film star. But of course his political career has made posters or Lobby Cards for *Bedtime For Bonzo* presidential memorabilia; scenes from his starring films, once available for under $5, fetched almost $100 for a title card ($40 for a scene) during his presidential campaign, and shot up to $300 when he was sworn in.

With dealers pack-ratting – collector's jargon for dealers who stockpile large quantities on films like *Star Wars, Chinatown, Raiders of the Lost Ark, Alien* etc. in the hope that these will be tomorrow's *Kong* or *Wizard of Oz* – the value of the old and the rare has just begun to be appreciated. But it's good to remember, there will always be a *Heaven's Gate*, and no one has ever yet truly fathomed the mind of a collector.

Meanwhile, for those who can't afford Lobby Cards at auctions or who simply enjoy looking at them, here is a selection of the best to remind one of a time when popcorn was 15 cents, a hot dog 9 cents, and the price of admission included a set of dishes.

FOYER PLEASURE

FOOLISH WIVES (U 1922), directed by Erich von Stroheim and starring von Stroheim, Mae Busch and Miss Du Pont, was considered to be a breakthrough in American movie making. It was the first 'adult' film, with its Jamesian theme of sexual relationships outside marriage, and the loss of American innocence (that of Miss Du Pont) through the irresistible allure of the decaying but ever glamorous old world of fading nobility (represented by von Stroheim). The construction of this set, extravagant, stylish and authentic down to the last pillar and palm, recreates Monte Carlo in all its shimmering splendor and was the focus of the movie's publicity campaign. The movie established von Stroheim's reputation as a director of genius, an actor you 'love to hate', and a profligate spendthrift.

ROSITA (UA 1923) was Ernst Lubitsch's first American film. Mary Pickford, who saw in his celebrated naturalistic European epics the chance for her to move out of child roles, brought Lubitsch from Berlin. The qualities that made him the master of the boudoir farce – delicacy, sophistication, innuendo – were only vaguely evident in his German spectaculars. *Rosita* and Mary Pickford, as a street singer in old Spain, failed to win the public's approval. Pickford returned to childhood parts and Lubitsch moved on to the bedroom farce. The magnificent sets were the work of Harold Grieves who became one of America's foremost interior decorators. Note that the Lobby Card here and on the previous page illustrates the film's key selling points.

MARY PICKFORD in "Rosita"

ZAZA (Par. 1923) was based on a 1904 French play by François Berton and Charles Simon. A successful boulevard melodrama, *Zaza* was played by almost every leading lady of the day, including Sarah Bernhardt, Geraldine Ferrar, Mrs Lesley Carter, David Belasco's famous star, and here in this Allan Dwan production Gloria Swanson. The story is Belle Epoque – sawdust and tears, backstage rivalries, dramas and heartbreaks. For this Lobby Card, Paramount's advertising department has ingeniously incorporated the style and feel of the nineteenth century French posters of Toulouse-Lautrec.

TRAPPED IN A SUBMARINE (British 1931). What's revealing about this image is the inventiveness of the men who were able to sell the American public on a British-made film without stars or the advance publicity that invariably accompanied a major American film during production. From this image it appears that the story has been torn from the headlines to create a sense of urgency and timeliness, an effect that is used to this day to sell exploitation films.

BIP AMERICA PRESENTS

"TRAPPED IN A SUBMARINE"

directed by WALTER SUMMERS

FE-SAVER FOR SUBMARINE CREW

ELLSBERG BELIEVES ALL DEAD ON M-2

MAY BE SUBMARINE

British Submarine Fails to Rise; Fifty-four Men on M-2 in Channel

The Davis Safety "Lung" Supplied to All... Sunken British Submarine

SCENE OF HUNT F...

BRITISH SHIPS HUNT SUBMARINE ALL DAY

SH SUBMARINE WITH 54 MEN

THE BLACK PIRATE (UA 1926) was one of the earliest of the three-strip technicolor films produced by a major Hollywood studio. To lure a moviegoing audience, Fairbanks' films did not need to go to the expense and complications of the color process which then required great care in design and composition. But Fairbanks was not simply interested in making movies (costume adventures full of his unique elan and boyish exuberance) for a pre-sold public but always tried to add to the wonder moving pictures inspired. He made movies he would have wanted to see. The cleverness here lies in the use of a silhouetted Fairbanks in the role he is loved for – athletic, vibrant, ready to carry us off on the road to adventure – and also to give us a glimpse of the thrills that await us in the hull of the Black Pirate's ship. Note that the story's action has been hinted at by imposing a cut-out of the ship – adventure, drama and design in one image.

DOUGLAS FAIRBANKS in *The* BLACK PIRATE

PHOTOGRAPHY IN TECHNICOLOR

DON JUAN (WB 1926). Directed by Alan Crosland. John Barrymore belonged to the triumvirate of 'great lovers of the silent screen'. (MGM had John Gilbert; Paramount, Valentino and Warner Brothers, with this story of the seventeenth century Spanish lover, Barrymore.) Mary Astor, the heroine, reclines; off-screen, she was in fact Barrymore's mistress. The pulled back curtain and the border at the top of the Lobby Card gives the illusion of an Old Master.

THE TEMPTRESS (MGM 1926). For Garbo's second American-made film the studio repeated all the key ingredients of her first: the same director, the same writer, another 'Latin lover' co-star and Garbo, yet again, a Spanish seductress – bold, provocative – the complete opposite of the Garbo she became. Note that the screenwriter is Dorothy Farnum; many of the most successful screenwriters in Hollywood were women and several of them wrote for Garbo. For the design of the Lobby Card, the poster artists took their cue from the film's title, posing her as for the figurehead on the prow of a ship, a Lorelei riding the crest of the wave inviting men to their doom; overhead, the pin-ups of her conquests show us her co-stars.

MONSIEUR BEAUCAIRE (Par. 1924). Rudolph Valenti-
no, the name above the title. The image selected for this card
looks more like a big screen close-up than a still, giving us a
provocative and heightened sense of his closeness to us. The
delicate hand in his could be that of any woman in the
audience, the eyes he is gazing into could be anyone's eyes.
The slight hand-tinting, the gold of his jacket, of his brooch,
and the simple golden band on her finger, adds a touch of the
erotic. The silhouette of an elegant young eighteenth century
courtier on the border of all the cards is a specially clever
touch. Silhouetting was a popular parlor amusement of the
eighteenth century, the time in which the story is set, as well
as being a step in the evolution of the movies.

LONDON AFTER MIDNIGHT (MGM 1927), casts Lon Chaney, 'the man of a thousand faces', whose films almost single-handedly launched a genre. This is a spoof of the horrible grotesques for which he was famous.

LON CHANEY
in
London After Midnight
with
ARCELINE DAY
ONRAD NAGEL
TOD BROWNING
PRODUCTION
Story by Tod Browning ~ Scenario by Waldemar Young ~ Titles by Joe Farnham ~ Directed by Tod Browning
A
Metro-Goldwyn-Mayer
PICTURE

WILLIAM HAINES

in

WEST POINT

A Metro-Goldwyn-Mayer PICTURE

"I thought you were mad at me."

MADE IN U.S.A.

WEST POINT (MGM 1928). William Haines (center) was the Robert Taylor, Van Johnson, Richard Chamberlain of his day at MGM, and one of the studio's most popular young stars. He was the boy mothers hoped their daughters would marry. Here he has just arrived at West Point – note the cadet cap; young Billy has a long way to go before he becomes one of the soldiers West Point can produce. When he left the film industry William Haines went on to become one of America's leading interior decorators.

THE FIRST KISS (Par. 1928). With this movie, one in a series, Paramount hoped to create a romantic team out of Fay Wray and Gary Cooper, a team of young lovers to rival the enormously popular Janet Gaynor and Charles Farrell. Five films later the studio dropped the idea; their rhythm as a romantic team was off. On the screen Fay Wray was perfect as the sweet little heroine – but not much more. Cooper seemed the sweet and decent boy, but projected a darker, deeper soul. In this title card for the film, inspired by the work of Charles Dana Gibson, the two appear perfectly matched. Note that Fay Wray's name appears before Gary Cooper's.

FAY WRAY AND GARY COOPER
IN
A Paramount Picture
'THE FIRST KISS'
Paramount Pictures
PARAMOUNT FAMOUS LASKY CORP.
A ROWLAND V. LEE PRODUCTION
FROM THE STORY "FOUR BROTHERS" BY TRISTRAM TUPPER ~~ ADAPTATION AND SCREEN PLAY BY JOHN FARROW
COUNTRY OF ORIGIN U. S. A.
THIS LOBBY DISPLAY LEASED FROM PARAMOUNT FAMOUS LASKY CORPORATION.

OUR DANCING DAUGHTERS (MGM 1928). Here is Joan Crawford as one of *Our Dancing Daughters* before life, time and her daughter turned her into one of our terrible mothers. Joan had gone from scrubbing floors and dancing in chorus lines to the top of the MGM heap in a series of films like this which made her the embodiment of the 'jazz age'. 'Tonight she would be gay.' And as C. B. de Mille would say, 'So it is written. So let it be done.' Joan, seen here on the table top, is the essential John Held flapper – one of the jazz age good-time kids. Time and fashion may change, youth never. The blue stenciled border of musical notes carries on the theme of hearts pounding to a jazz rhythm. Joan is doing what everybody out there wants to do – be free, young and have a good time. The danger and excitement of reckless behavior is carried through in the colors selected by the art department – the loud, bold red which frames the small stencil-colored still is picked up in Joan's dress, adding to the sense of abandonment.

AFTER MIDNIGHT (MGM 1927). Norma Shearer and Joan Crawford were two of the rising stars who came in the wake of Garbo and Clara Bow – young, free, and uninhibited. Shearer is soon to be Mrs Thalberg, and the uncrowned Queen of MGM – but already she was a favorite with the public. In *After Midnight*, Norma plays a young girl caught up in a tug of war with the dangers that await a modern-day Cinderella. The scene probably took place in a living room, but to heighten the drama, it has been superimposed against an enormous clock. The size of Shearer's name and the fact that it had to be mentioned in all publicity clearly establishes her as a box office draw. The line of dialogue, 'Mary, you mustn't!' may have been one of the titles in the film, and could have been said by either the man or the woman pulling on her.

When HALLELUJAH! (MGM 1929) was made, it was rare for a director's name to appear above the title of the picture, and almost never by itself. But the Texas-born King Vidor had given the public a series of popular and critically acclaimed films. This was King Vidor's first talkie as well as being the first all-black feature-length film. It's clear from this unsigned but unusually beautiful piece of poster art that the studio knew they had something special, and were trying to launch it with the dignity of a Broadway stage production. One has to admire MGM for producing this movie at a time when there was little hope of it playing anywhere in the south, and the likelihood of it doing much in the north wasn't all that great.

THE CANARY MURDER CASE (Par. 1929). It was because of this film that Louise Brooks' career came to an end. The film was shot as a silent picture just before Louise went off to Europe to become the legendary Lulu. When she returned, enlightened and inspired from her work with Pabst, she was told that Paramount was dubbing the picture for sound and that she would have to dub her part. She refused. The studio hired Margaret Livingstone to dub Louise's voice, and dropped Louise. They made it clear to all contract players that any star could be replaced, no matter how big. While Louise Brooks was revealed as an extraordinary presence in German and French films, it is ironic that she, in fact, never looked more astonishingly beautiful than in this American movie which cost her her Hollywood career. The Philo Vance series, based on the works of S.S. Van Dine, was instrumental in altering another career, that of William Powell, who went from playing villains and second leads to romantic starring roles. The Canary here, a term popularized by Damon Runyan for the squeaky chanteuses who work shady nightclubs, is Louise. She sits on the 'C'; note the hand coming out of the '*a*nary'.

SUNNY SIDE UP (Fox 1929) was the eagerly anticipated talkie debut of America's sweethearts. Garbo and Gilbert were America's erotic fantasy; Colman and Banky, exalted romance; and Gaynor and Farrell, love's young dream. Clearly this was a prestigious film, and the importance attached to it is evident here in the lightness and elegance of the design. Note the signature of the designer on bottom left; the studio got the very best. *Sunny Side Up* was one of Hollywood's first and most original musicals, with a score by the distinguished team of De Sylva, Brown and Henderson, whose hits included the title song for Jolson's *Sonny Boy*.

WILD PARTY (Par. 1929) was the celebrated 'It Girl's talkie debut. Clara Bow at that time was the studio's hottest property. She was young, her fame had come upon her too fast, her private life was a publicized mess, and making this talking picture, which terrified her, drew her ever closer to the inevitable breakdown she suffered the following year.

Clara Bow was so enormously popular that her films were titled more for her public image than for the story. Bow could have become as big as Garbo, who entered the sound era with an already extraordinarily potent image which was enhanced by the quality of her voice; the tremendous vitality that Clara Bow projected on the screen combined with the quality of her voice to create an even more complex range and depth. Her co-star, fresh from Broadway success, doesn't even get billing here; in 1929 a Clara Bow picture needed only the Clara Bow name. Three years later, Clara had left the screen for ever, and Frederic March was one of Hollywood's most popular stars.

Clara
BOW
"The
WILD PARTY"

A Paramount Picture

"DON'T BE FRIGHTENED—I'LL DEAL WITH THOSE ROUGHNECKS"

2857 - "COUNTRY OF ORIGIN U.S.A."

THIS ONLY DISPLAY LEASED FROM PARAMOUNT FAMOUS LASKY CORP.

INDISCREET (UA 1931). Five years and six movies (including the aborted *Queen Kelly* directed by Erich von Stroheim) after Swanson had declined Paramount's extraordinarily lavish offer of a guaranteed $1,000,000 a year, to go independent with United Artists, her career, despite a personal triumph in her talkie debut, had entered the doldrums. Her life up to then was, for the public who adored her, a fairy tale of the 1920s, the young girl made into a star by de Mille. Swanson was a mere 32, her image was still good but new faces like Joan Crawford, Norma Shearer and Garbo were coming up. The lettering of the Lobby Card deliberately plays up Swanson's name, and the film's title hints at her private life, though in a good, clean modern way: SWANSON – INDISCREET. It's the comedienne they are playing up, not the clothes horse. The studio has a big star whose name is the single biggest draw but whose last few films have been flops, and here they are trying to offer a new, fresh (clean) Swanson. Note that the film's producers are the hugely successful song-writing team of De Sylva, Brown and Henderson (see also page 53, *Sunny Side Up*).

RESURRECTION

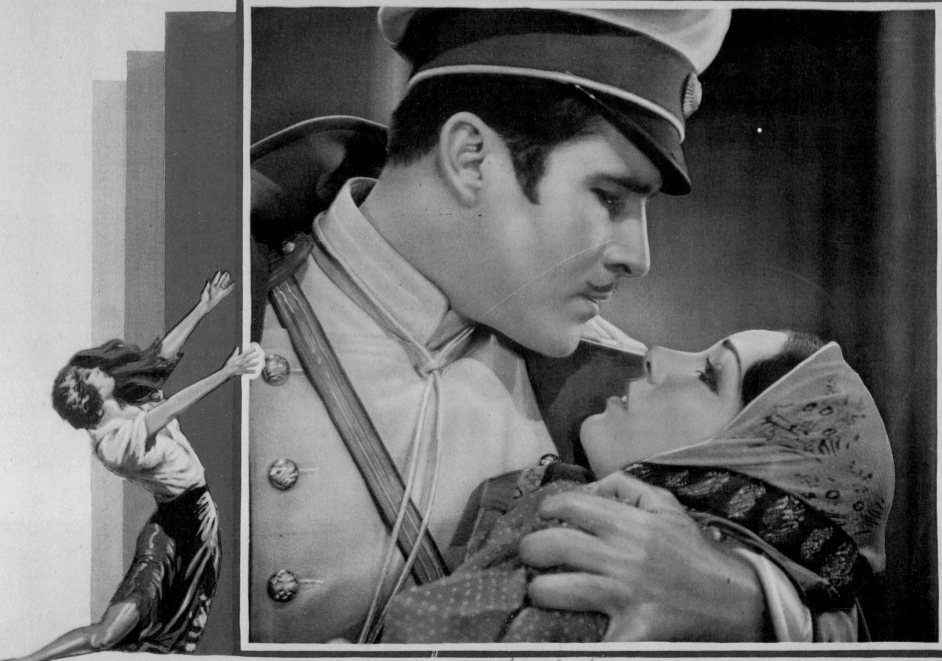

a universal picture

RESURRECTION. Tolstoy's great novel had already been filmed several times as a silent picture, the last one only a few years earlier with Dolores Del Rio, before this first of several talkies, released by Universal in 1931. The illustration of the imploring woman on the border appears on all the cards for this movie. The scenes depicted may vary but her stance is used to symbolize the central theme of this version of the story. She loves him steadfastly despite his betrayal of her and her subsequent downfall. The still here shows John Boles and Lupe Velez – both beautiful, romantic, unreachable and ideal – the opposite of life, where the beautiful girl goes for the plain man, or the intellectual takes up with the dumb blonde. But in movies the handsome hero meets and falls in love with the lovely heroine and while in life they'd probably be a washout in bed, on the screen they are the perfect couple, something to set off the fantasies of their public. The deco border adds a stylish period touch, not unlike the designs of the movie theatres of the day.

HELL'S ANGELS (UA 1930) was Howard Hughes' first film as a director. It was begun in the last days of the silent era, but work on it was scrapped when sound came in to take advantage of the potential of the new medium – the roar of planes taking off, the fire of machine guns in the World War I aerial battles. Hughes also wanted a new leading lady to replace the Swedish actress Greta Nissen, whose accent he considered unsuitable for the role of a British socialite loved by two pilots. Hughes' discovery became more famous than the film itself. But at the time of the film's release, Jean Harlow's name meant nothing to the public. The emphasis here is on the war, and the money it cost to recreate it, cashing in on the success of one of the silent era's last great war epics, *Wings*. This is a daunting but triumphant image; the planes were not a clever mock-up but came from an actual scene in the film (for once, what one saw is what one got, a sky obliterated by avenging angels). The title, ironically, describes what will become the image of the new star – the first great sex symbol of the sound era. For the film's 1937 reissue, this Lobby Card had been changed; by that time Harlow had risen to the pinnacle of stardom. On the original lobby and poster art her name would have appeared in the same sized type as that of the two established male stars, and below theirs.

THE LOVE PARADE (Par. 1929) was one of the first and still the most celebrated of the musicals produced in the early years of 'talkies'. It was Ernst Lubitsch's eagerly awaited sound debut, Chevalier's follow-up to his sensational first American film *Innocents of Paris* released earlier the same year, and Jeanette MacDonald's film debut.

The design of the card, particularly in its use of colors, resembles the style of nineteenth century postcards, with an almost 3-dimensional effect created by stencil printing, the colors rather boldly and somewhat slapdashedly applied but conveying the lightness and humor of the original stage musical, *The Prince Consort*, by Jean Xanrof and Jules Chancel. The strongest visual points in the lettering are Chevalier's and Lubitsch's names, which were synonymous in the public's mind with lightheartedness, wit, style, sophistication and good clean sex.

WEREWOLF OF LONDON (U 1935). The studio that had brought us *Dracula* (1930), *Frankenstein* (1931) and *The Mummy* (1932), added a *Werewolf* to keep the box office dollars rolling in and the studio out of bankruptcy. The film has no star names such as Karloff or Lugosi, nor does the promotion. The promise of terror sold the picture; the public didn't really care who played the werewolf at the bottom of the staircase (the distinguished stage actor Henry Hull in his film debut), or that the mysterious figure in mid-air was Warner Oland, popular in his role as the Oriental detective Charlie Chan. It's an intriguing image, with the fantasy element indicated by the ghostlike spectre towering over London's Big Ben, heightened by the use of super-imposition.

WHITE WOMAN (Par. 1933). The hand tinted colors are a lurid attempt to place the lovers (Carole Lombard and Kent Taylor) in a Rousseauesque jungle – suggesting an Eden for primitive passions. Charles Laughton was fresh from his screen triumphs as the sadistic scientist in *The Island of Lost Souls*, and as an outrageously flamboyant homosexual Nero in *The Sign of the Cross*, as well as a whole gallery of other perverse, tormented, and tormenting characters. Here he plays another. Lombard, still several years away from her emergence as the queen of screwball comedy, was fresh from her substitute Dietrich, substitute Harlow, substitute Bankhead, substitute Constance Bennett triumphs as the studio's favorite all-purpose substitute glamor puss. Kent Douglas, with Lombard in the boat, was, along with Cary Grant, Randolph Scott and Ray Milland, one of the studio's hopeful future stars.

FRANKENSTEIN (U 1931) was the calculated follow-up to the enormously successful *Dracula*, which the studio had made the year before, and which had helped to keep it solvent. Both films established the horror film as a genre. Here, Colin Clive, Mae Clarke, John Boles and Boris Karloff were names but not stars (Universal didn't have stars). The image here of Frankenstein's monster is like a circus tiger first seen leaping through a flaming hoop. In a style reminiscent of German Expressionism (most of the Universal employees were German, so that isn't surprising) the monster is like an angry god who bursts through the heavens to wreak his vengeance on the earthlings below, and the virgin bride, who comes in the shadows, is a sacrifice prepared to appease him. By accentuating certain parts of the monster's body – the hand and foot – the artist creates a sense of menace.

CARL LAEMMLE
presents
FRANKENSTEIN
THE MAN WHO MADE A MONSTER!
with
COLIN CLIVE ◦ MAE CLARKE
JOHN BOLES ◦ BORIS KARLOFF
DWIGHT FRYE
EDWARD VAN SLOAN
and FREDERIC KERR
Based upon the story by
MARY WOLLSTONECROFT SHELLEY
ADAPTED BY
JOHN L. BALDERSTON
from the play by PEGGY WEBLING
DIRECTED BY
JAMES WHALE
A UNIVERSAL PICTURE
PRODUCED BY
CARL LAEMMLE, JR.

DISHONORED (Par. 1931). Dietrich calling the tune in her second American-made film, which, like Morocco, her first with von Sternberg, is centred around her personality. Dietrich dominates the encircling men, as she does the movie. The man playing opposite her could have been any one of the studio's male stars, and Victor McLaglen, better known as an Irish bruiser in John Ford films than a romantic lead, was simply the man available at the time. Nevertheless here he gets top billing due to his existing contract with the studio. The image invites the audience to discover for themselves the true meaning of the title, *Dishonored*.

TARZAN AND HIS MATE (MGM 1934) was the second in the fabulously successful MGM series based on the adventures of Edgar Rice Burroughs' ape man. The first film released the year before had established Olympic swimming champion Johnny Weismuller as a star to be reckoned with, as well as typecasting him. In the public's mind, Tarzan was Weismuller, despite several concurrent and subsequent actors in the role. The mate referred to, actress Maureen O'Sullivan who stands beside him and who co-starred in the first six of the Tarzan films as his Jane, is not even mentioned here on the logo. Her scanty costume in this film caused a great furor among the censors.

ROMAN SCANDALS (UA 1933) was a typically lavish Eddie Cantor–Goldwyn musical with spectacular musical numbers. Among the girls chained up on the top tier of the auction block, about to be sold to the highest bidder at the Roman slave market, is Lucille Ball. This somewhat surrealistic number climaxes with a young girl horrified at having been sold to a fat old Roman, running to the top of the Roman cake and leaping to her death, while below Ruth Etting sings the blues. Musicals such as this were modeled on the formula established by the legendary Flo Ziefeld: lavish costumes, sets, and gorgeous girls surrounding the antics of a popular comedian. In the 1940s many of the Cantor vehicles were handed down to Danny Kaye.

THE LOST SQUADRON (RKO 1932). Art sometimes gets uncomfortably close to life; this is a case in point. The title refers to the aimless, unemployed World War I daredevil fighter pilots who, because of the depression, are reduced to risking life and limb at fairground exhibitions, and as stunt pilots in Hollywood war dramas like *Wings, The Legion of the Condemned, Hell's Angels* (see page 61). At the heart of the story is one of those pilots (Richard Dix) who finds work in one of those movies directed by a megalomaniac Teutonic Hollywood director who'll do anything for a good scene, even if it costs the lives of a few extras. This 'inside Hollywood' revelation capitalized on several events which had recently shocked the American public; the reported deaths of the stunt men working in the aforementioned dramas, particularly the Hughes' epic; the casting of Erich von Stroheim, publicized as 'the man you love to hate', in the role of the sadistic director von Furst, the man you *had* to hate. The public thought they were getting a slice of the 'real' Hollywood, the hot bed of sex, sin and violence. Note the illustration on the bottom right border of the crew filming, von Stroheim as the director.

THE LOST SQUADRON

RKO RADIO PICTURE

MADE IN U.S.A

BLONDE VENUS (Par. 1932) was Dietrich's fourth film with Josef von Sternberg and with it the studio hoped to erase the failure of her previous film (*Song of Songs*) which was not directed by von Sternberg. Dietrich is so big, her name so prominently displayed, that she *is* the film. It is called *Blonde Venus* because the movie has to have a title for identification purposes, but what does Blonde Venus mean? The still here is very beautiful – of course the lighting is von Sternberg's. The graphics are basically simple and reveal the extravagant nature of the film.

NAGANA (U 1933). The studio spent a fortune promoting Tala Birell as their exotic Garboesque-Dietrich-like new star from Europe, but note that her name appears nowhere on the card of her first starring film. The artwork here is in the style of the old circus poster – savage beasts in furious conflict who even overwhelm the pair of romantic lovers, and supposedly the stars of the picture, Tala and Melvyn Douglas. It's possible that after the studio had seen the picture they decided to go with the animals rather than Tala. Thereafter she appeared in supporting roles, and soon sank from sight, but not before she appeared in Josef von Sternberg's (creator of the Dietrich personae) *Crime and Punishment*. Tala's rapid rise and fall was one of those unfortunate examples of the studio's attempt to recreate the image of another star. Like Gwili Andrew, Anna Stenn and Marta Labarr, Tala, who was a fine actress, would have been better off if she hadn't been forced into the Garbo mold.

CARL LAEMMLE presents

"NAGANA"

a UNIVERSAL picture

COUNTRY OF ORIGIN U. S. A.

For the film's release the title was altered to read, simply, BOMBSHELL (MGM 1933). Amusingly enough, Mae West, Paramount's own 'Blonde Bombshell', had been approached by MGM to provide material for Harlow. The script for this popular spoof on the life of Hollywood sex-star Lola Burns was modeled on Harlow's own image, with the additional in-joke that Lola's grasping greedy family was almost a duplicate of Harlow's. In this comedy, Lola Burns runs away from the pressures of Hollywood and family; the 'Prince Charming' she runs away with turns out to be just another opportunist. In the end, pursued by her wisecracking press agent (played by Lee Tracy), Lola sees Hollywood in a more positive light. The screenplay for this farce was by Jules Furthman, author of many of Marlene Dietrich's most famous films (*Morocco, Dishonored, Shanghai Express*), and John Lee Mahin. Mahin was sufficiently intimate with Harlow at the time to draw on Harlow's own life for his script. Harlow was just 26 when she died in 1937.

The background for this scene from the film has been simplified for the Lobby Card to emphasize the stars. Note that the artwork bordering the image suggests fireworks – the promise of ninety minutes of fun.

I'M NO ANGEL (Par. 1933) was Mae West's third film. It follows *She Done Him Wrong* which saved Paramount from bankruptcy. Mae was in her forties when she hit Hollywood after a triumphant career on Broadway as playwright and star, and innumerable tangles with the law and moral reformers for plays like *Sex, Drag* and the production that became a theatrical landmark, *Diamond Lil*. In *She Done Him Wrong*, a heavily toned-down version of her *Diamond Lil*, Mae West set the country aflame, and became the highest priced star in Hollywood. With *I'm No Angel*, a contemporary sex-comedy, the publicity department reminds the public of her last romp. So closely was she identified in the public's mind with this Rabelaisian nineties' heroine that she appears in full costume from the previous film. (In her contract it stated that Mae West had to appear full-figure in all the advertising.) Her name overshadows the film's title, the name of the studio, and that of her co-star; if the movie had been called *Tillie of the Floss* it wouldn't have mattered. The public knew that if it starred Mae, a good time would be had by all. This is young Cary Grant's second film opposite Mae West; she had hand-picked him. (Rifling him with her eyes she had said, 'You can be had.') We all know the rest. It launched him on his lifelong love affair with the public.

QUEEN CHRISTINA (MGM 1933). This is the film that gave the world the unforgettable image of Garbo, standing alone, untouchable, on the prow of the ship, sailing to meet her destiny. The film (directed by Rouben Mamoulian) about the seventeenth century Swedish bachelor-Queen who renounced her throne for a life of exile would prove prophetic for the Swedish actress. The film, the studio's most prestigious production for the year, brought Garbo back to Hollywood to continue the career she had often thought of renouncing. It was not the hoped-for success; her character embodied what the public had already begun to resist: Garbo's remoteness. During the remaining seven years she spent in Hollywood, Garbo made six more films. *Ninotchka* was the only popular triumph, though all of them made her as a star beyond reach. Today that world has disappeared but the image of Garbo remains.

Garbo

QUEEN CHRISTINA

A Metro Goldwyn Mayer PICTURE

COUNTRY OF ORIGIN U.S.A.

JIMMY THE GENT (WB 1934). Cagney had become a meteoric star par excellence four years earlier in *The Public Enemy*. As the gangster-hero, a new type (anti-social, violent, self-sufficient) was launched. By 1934, a change in moral attitudes demanded a new Cagney image. The qualities that had made him so popular as the lone wolf the nation's youth could identify with (as the youth of another generation would with James Dean) were now redirected. Cagney went from comedy-spoofs like this to crime fighters, and finally became a star beyond type casting. To appreciate how extraordinary the transition was one has only to look at the career of Marilyn Monroe, who for all her enormous popularity was never able to escape her image and keep her public. As part of Cagney's transitional stage, we are given here a light-hearted cartoon image. The title says it all – not about the film but about the new Cagney. The Lobby Card has a Damon Runyanesque feel to it. That same year Bette Davis, an industrious actress, would catapult to a stardom equal to Cagney's, as Mildred in *Of Human Bondage*. Here she's just a foil for Cagney.

GOLD DIGGERS IN PARIS (WB 1938) was the fifth and last of the Gold Diggers series. Although the lavish production numbers were still choreographed by Busby Berkeley they, like the film itself, were no longer memorable. The cheerful though grasping good-natured blonde was no longer appealing. What's most interesting about this card is the design which spotlights 'The Great White Way' (of New York?) in Folies Bergère Paris.

THE WHITE PARADE (Fox 1934) celebrates the nurses who devote their lives to the care of others. Loretta Young, who had just come to Fox from Warner Brothers and an endless succession of roles as the pretty but vacuous heroine, is given the chance to act the sort of role played by Kay Francis, Barbara Stanwyck, or even Bette Davis. But the public preferred Loretta as the famous star and the studio put her in their frothy comedies. Here they are putting across the seriousness of the subject: the nurses marching as soldiers, linked in their fight against illness, misery and disease, and Loretta, as one of the valiant fighters, renouncing her own concerns for the greater good. The colors here, low key, antiseptic, would be suitable for an ad for bandaids.

THE WHITE PARADE

A JESSE LASKY PRODUCTION

with *Loretta* YOUNG ★ *John* BOLES

Directed by IRVING CUMMINGS · FOX PICTURE

The "Svengali woman", shrunken to doll's size, sets out on her master's errand of vengeance!

THE **DEVIL DOLL** STARRING LIONEL BARRYMORE

A Metro-Goldwyn-Mayer PICTURE

THE DEVIL DOLL (MGM 1936). Tod Browning established his reputation for the macabre by directing most of Lon Chaney's famous silent horror films, as well as *Dracula*, the first of them to launch the genre in the thirties, and the legendary *Freaks*. He was here at the end of his career with this B budget, no-star, very peculiar movie. A man disguised as an elderly woman (played by Lionel Barrymore) uses a formula to shrink people to wreak his vengeance on those who destroyed his life.

CRACK-UP (Fox 1936). With B pictures, contractual agreements about names, credits and size of type were not of prime importance, and the poster artists had greater freedom to be inventive. This illustration could be from any pulp magazine of the period but shows as well the influence of the serious artists of the period – Thomas Hart Benton and other WPA artists. The action takes place on a passenger plane pre-dating *Airport* by forty years.

CRACK-UP

PETER LORRE
BRIAN DONLEVY
HELEN WOOD
RALPH MORGAN
THOMAS BECK

ASSOCIATE PRODUCER
SAMUEL G. ENGEL

DIRECTED BY
MALCOLM
ST. CLAIR

20th CENTURY FOX

A 20TH CENTURY-FOX PICTURE

B

AFTER OFFICE HOURS (MGM 1935). Clark Gable, hot after his Oscar winning success in *It Happened One Night*, has been elevated to top billing with Constance Bennett in the kind of woman-orientated picture in which he previously supported stars like Crawford, Shearer, Garbo and Bennett herself. Thereafter, with only a few exceptions (Shearer, Crawford) Gable received top billing. Constance Bennett was loathed (by the studio) and admired (by her fellow stars) as reputedly one of the shrewdest businesswomen among actresses, negotiating contracts which at the peak of her fashionable popularity in the early thirties (spawning a series of art deco-blondes like Carole Lombard and Bette Davis) earned her the highest weekly wage in movies and the freedom to make films for other studios in her holiday periods, with the full salary going to her and not her parent studio. By 1935 her vogue and period of top stardom was over, and a move to MGM failed to revitalize her career, though she continued making films for the rest of her life, lending glamor and a stylish sparkle to her work. As with *After Midnight* (see page 46), time was the key element of this Lobby Card, in the form of the large clock handles framing the still and pointing to the trap (or delights) that await honest office girls (and boys) when work turns to play in the boss's apartment.

Clark GABLE AND Constance BENNETT

IN "AFTER OFFICE HOURS

A Metro-Goldwyn-Mayer PICTURE

" You're the kind of person you dream about -- but never expect to meet!"

COUNTRY OF ORIGIN U.S.A.

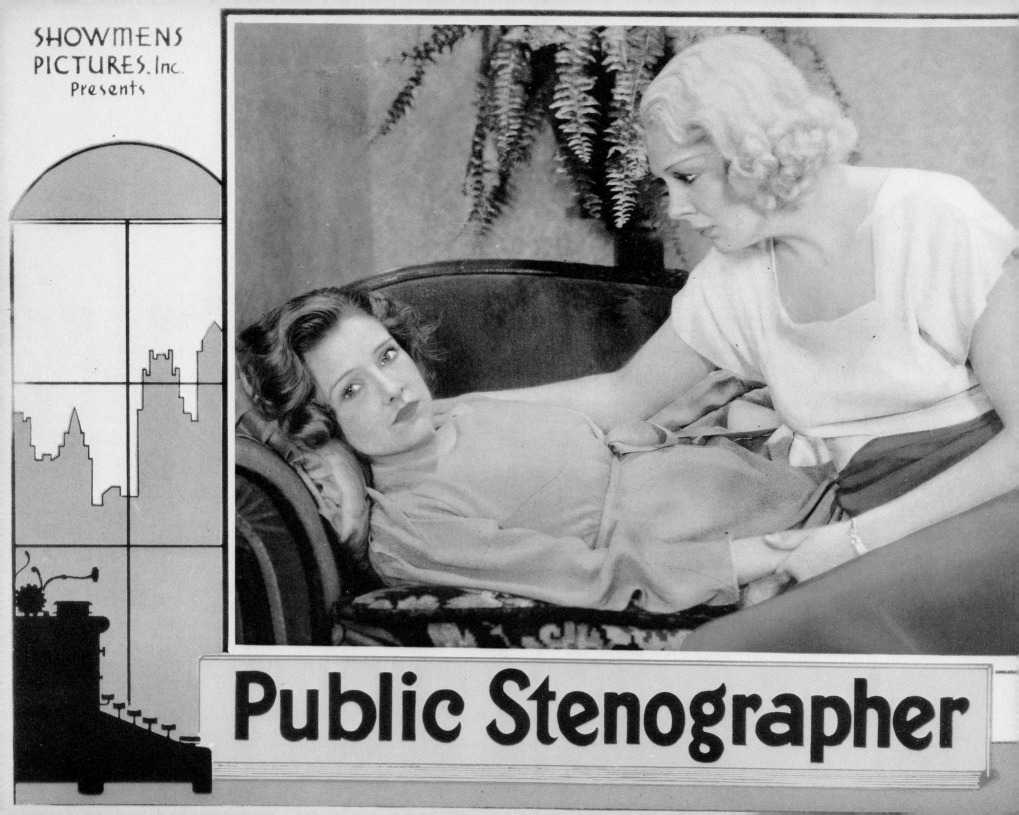

PUBLIC STENOGRAPHER (SP Inc.-Mac 1934). Here is an interesting bit of design: the typewriter in the border, the big city skyline behind it, and the still that shows two women, one who appears heartbroken, as if she's just heard the bad news, and her pal, the blonde, probably a loose (because she's a dyed blonde) but good-hearted soul (because all dyed blondes were) who comforts her. There are no stars, no names, not even a studio logo, but it does have something – pizazz!

BECKY SHARP (RKO 1935) was an eighty-three minute version of Thackeray's novel, *Vanity Fair*. It was the first feature in three-color Technicolor, and Rouben Mamoulian's color design was ravishing. To show the brilliance of the film's colors here, in the still, they have heightened the reds of the uniforms, the gold of her dress and her hair, and, most important, the delicate coloring of her skin. By the use of big prestige names like Miriam Hopkins and director Rouben Mamoulian, color was not to be a box-office gimmick but a serious element in Hollywood's future productions. Miriam Hopkins is the center of a period decoration, in which the Wellington emblem flanks the French *fleur de lis* for the culmination of the story in the Battle of Waterloo.

BECKY SHARP

A ROUBEN MAMOULIAN PRODUCTION

SARATOGA (MGM 1937) was a fashionable American race track (revealed by the artwork lower left) but the film's title couldn't have meant much outside America, unlike the title *Monte Carlo* which immediately conjures up to an international audience – glamor, money, excitement, fast cars and beautiful women (the style of the logo here might have given a clue). From this, one sees how Lobby Cards helped sell films to the public. Harlow died during the making of the movie, necessitating the use of a double for the remaining footage. That the film is a footnote in the history of the cinema has little to do with its merits and everything to do with her untimely death. No amount of artistic embellishment or manipulation can say as much as the evident rapport between these two. (Harlow's character was similar to Gable's – wise-cracking, straight shooting, a pal and a lover.)

DESIRE (Par. 1936) was Marlene Dietrich's first film after her professional working relationship with director Josef von Sternberg was finished, and reunites her with Gary Cooper, the star of her first American film, *Morocco*. *Desire* is a delightful sophisticated romantic comedy remake of the German film of a few years earlier, and was directed by Frank Borzage, one of the masters of the genre. This posed, stylized image doesn't reveal the true nature of the film (Marlene is one of a band of jewel thieves) but the artwork in the border, common in popular romantic magazines of the day, tells us a modern love story awaits. Although Gary Cooper, along with Gable and Cagney, was one of the biggest box office draws in Hollywood, the thirties was the age of the 'woman's picture and the woman stars' and everything about this Lobby Card reiterates that – the image selected, the artwork on the side, and the title.

ADOLPH ZUKOR PRESENTS

MARLENE DIETRICH and GARY COOPER

in

'Desire,'

A Paramount Picture

JOHN HALLIDAY · WILLIAM FRAWLEY · ERNEST COSSART · AKIM TAMIROFF · ALAN MOWBRAY Directed by Frank Borzage
From a comedy by Hans Szekely and R. A. Stemmle

SYLVIA SCARLETT (RKO 1935) was an eccentric comedy about gender confusion, a comic device popular since the renaissance but not always successful in films, where the camera might reveal more than the people involved, and the public who came to see the latest Katharine Hepburn film, had in mind. Hepburn's attractively boyish quality in her straight roles, which added a sexual ambiguity and allure, was lost when she played in *Sylvia Scarlett*. The image here, if one had not seen the film, would suggest to the public that something was about to transpire between the sluttish woman in bed and the boy who was Katharine Hepburn in disguise. The suggestiveness was too much for 1935 and only turned the public away. The director was George Cukor; Hepburn's leading man was Cary Grant.

A YANK AT OXFORD (MGM 1938). Robert Taylor was the romantic idol of the moment. When MGM opened a branch of their studios in England, they used Robert Taylor to star in their first British-made film. Much of the film was to be shot in historic English locations, but the crowd that turned out to meet him wouldn't go away and it became necessary to film most of it in the newly built studios. The film's leading lady was Tarzan's Jane, the pretty Maureen O'Sullivan, but another actress in a small part would outshine them all, Vivien Leigh, who was to co-star with Taylor in the film that was her own favorite, *Waterloo Bridge*. *Yank*'s success launched MGM's British operations successfully, and resulted in a sequel starring Mickey Rooney.

"I wish we could be to-gether... like this... always!"

Robert *Taylor*

A *Yank* AT OXFORD

A Metro-Goldwyn-Mayer PICTURE

COUNTRY OF ORIGIN U. S. A.

LOST HORIZON (Col. 1937). The title comes out at us as if from nowhere. Frank Capra was a hugely successful director at this time; Ronald Colman was one of the most popular of stars. But what dominates all is the title, opening up for us the splendors and tranquility of Shangri La. In the border, Jane Wyatt, Ronald Colman and Margo; behind them the sun, symbolizing hope, resurrection, life – a theme repeated in the type and colors of the title. Because of the enormous success of the book due to the utopian dream it promised a beleagured world, everyone involved, stars, director, took second billing to the title. The James Hilton fantastical palace in the sky was inspired by the creations of Frank Lloyd Wright.

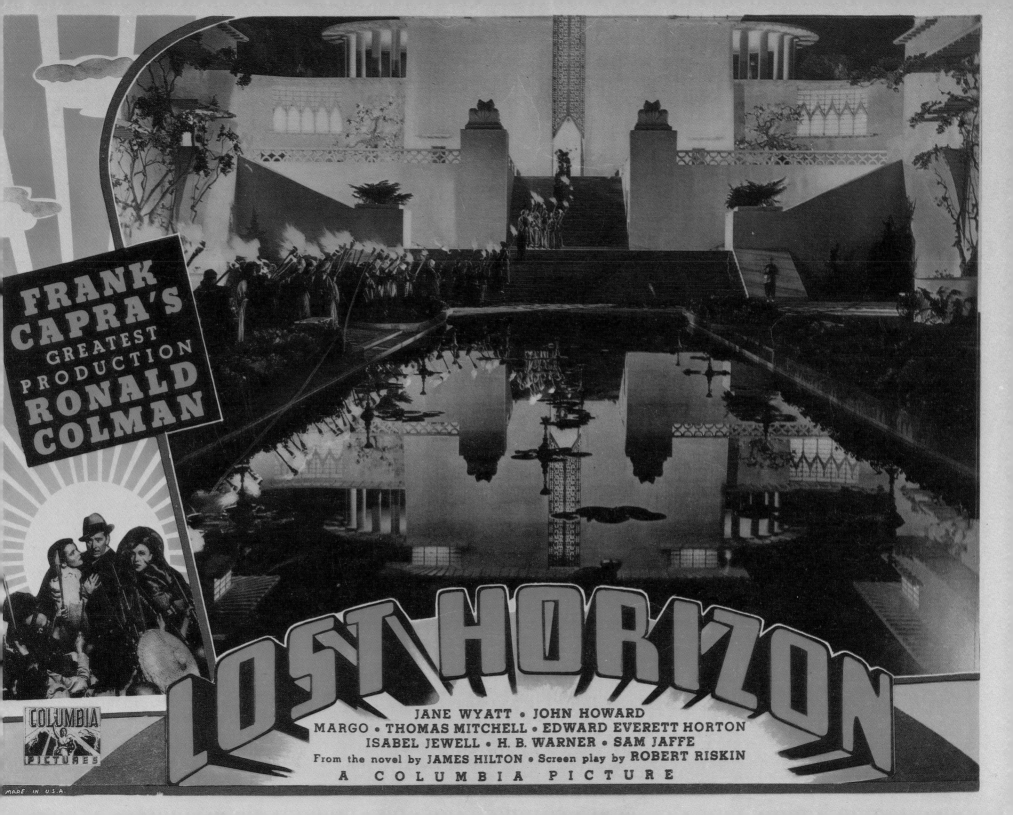

I FOUND STELLA PARRISH (WB 1935). Films such as this one had established Kay Francis as the glamorous, highly paid Queen of the Soap Opera movies. Two years later the studio, sensing that she was slipping at the box office, wanted to buy out her contract. When she refused, they put her in a slew of low budget B films until her contract ran out, and by then her career was ruined.

A FIRST NATIONAL PRODUCTIONS CORPORATION PICTURE
KAY FRANCIS IN
I FOUND STELLA PARISH

BROADWAY MELODY OF 1938 (MGM 1937). The first *Broadway Melody* was made in 1929 (the first talking picture to win an Oscar, and the only musical to win one for the next thirty years). The second *Broadway Melody* was of 1936, and turned Eleanor Powell, the tap-dancing kid from Broadway, into a spectacular new star. MGM's art director, Cedric Gibbons, was able to create some of his most ingenious, spectacular, and lush sets for these happy-go-mindless musical revues. Of course, a set like this, originally built for *Dancing Lady* (1933), Joan Crawford's last and most splendiforously designed musical, would not be allowed to waste away in the prop department, and so, rearranged, turned upside down or placed against different backdrops, it would be reused in different films. It reappeared in numerous MGM musicals with the public none the wiser.

Robert TAYLOR AND Eleanor POWELL IN
Broadway Melody of 1938
A METRO-GOLDWYN-MAYER PICTURE

The gorgeous Mirror of Lovely Girls number!

BRINGING UP BABY (RKO 1938) marked the end of the screwball craze. The threat of war was everywhere. The public wanted their stars to behave seriously; they wanted children to be like children and adults to behave like adults. They were no longer amused by the problems of the flighty, scatterbrained heiress, or the man who couldn't cope with practical life, let alone the one who dressed in drag and ran around backyards digging up bones. This film, which critics like Pauline Kael have called 'the cinema's closest equivalent to Restoration Comedy', was not a success, and Katharine Hepburn went back to Broadway to star in a new play, *The Philadelphia Story*. The madcap flavor of this sophisticated 'New York' smart comedy was summed up in the cartoon, which was in the style of the old humor magazine, *Life*, and was lifted from the poster for the film.

TOY WIFE (MGM 1938). Zoe Akins, author and mistress of hoop-skirted sentiment (*The Old Maid*), successful Broadway playwright (*The Greeks Had A Word For It*) and one of Hollywood's highest priced writers (*Camille, Zaza*) was given the task (or at least the credit) of providing two time Oscar winning Viennese import Luise Rainer with a glamorous vehicle. Miss Rainer's Oscars, two years in succession (for her role of Flo Ziegfeld's discarded wife, Anna Held, in *The Great Ziegfeld*, and the pathetic O-lan, the discarded wife in *The Good Earth*), created an Oscar landmark never repeated. *The Toy Wife* was a Frou Frou ante-bellum flirt in the Scarlett/Jezebel tradition, and provided Miss Rainer with two leading men vying for her favor. But *Frou Frou*, the film's original title, was all that the film offered, and ninety minutes of a frivolous Miss Rainer struggling to hide tears behind winsome smiles – and vice versa – was icing without the cake. While one can hardly accuse the studio of losing faith in Rainer's drawing power at this point, the film, with refurbished sets and costumes from MGM's storehouse (the lavish staircase came from *Operator 13*, etc.), the assignment of Richard (haste without taste) Thorpe, to direct, and Merian C. Cooper (who gave the world *King Kong*) as producer, hardly augurs the total commitment and concern this sort of subject would have needed to succeed. In its way, the poster graphics, in the style of the Bauhaus, were also out of step with the high romance of the subject. The film's failure, coupled with Miss Rainer's iron-willed temperament, marked the turning point of her career. In her next film, the opulent *Great Waltz*, she was, once again, back as the discarded wife. But this time there was no Oscar for her suffering, and nobody cared.

Luise RAINER as The TOY WIFE

with Melvyn DOUGLAS

Robert YOUNG

Barbara H.B.
O'NEIL · WARNER

Screen Play by ZOE AKINS · Directed by RICHARD THORPE
Produced by MERIAN C. COOPER

A Metro-Goldwyn-Mayer PICTURE

COUNTRY OF ORIGIN U. S. A.

TELEVISION SPY (Par. 1939). When this (now prophetic) film was released by Paramount in 1939, it seemed to be the sort of programmer studios churned out to boost a bill, at little expense to themselves, to offer the moviegoing public more value for their money. In the 1940s, the subject of television as a malevolent influence was to appear in fiction. And just as the artists of film posters may possibly have influenced budding pop-artists with ideas of color, design etc., so too may they have influenced writers. Ray Bradbury, in his short story *The Veldt*, published in the 1940s, writes of a family who, watching a jungle story on their television console, are swallowed up by the animals on the screen. Little could Hollywood have known the real menace television would become for movies, when it burst forth and swallowed up their public.

TELEVISION SPY

with
WILLIAM HENRY · JUDITH BARRETT · WILLIAM COLLIER, Sr. · ANTHONY QUINN · RICHARD DENNING
DIRECTED BY EDWARD DMYTRYK   SCREEN PLAY BY HORACE McCOY, WILLIAM R. LIPMAN and LILLIE HAYWARD   A PARAMOUNT PICTURE

Paramount Pictures

THE COWBOY AND THE LADY (UA 1938) was from an original story by Leo McCarey, Hollywood's masterful director of romantic comedies (*Love Affair, The Awful Truth,* etc.). It used the popular screwball theme of 'the hick and the heiress' but, by setting it out west, and having it star Gary Cooper (America's favorite hick) they avoid the offputting theme of a high life, high class, who-cares milieu that had begun to grate on the public's nerves. To make sure the public doesn't mistake the film for a 'sophisticated comedy', the steer-wrestling cowboy in the lower left artwork and the lassoo-swirling cowboy coralling the center still, emphasize the common touch. Cooper was one of the highest priced male stars in the business, and roles like 'Longfellow' Deeds (champion of the underdog) had given him a place in the mind of the public along with the likes of Abraham Lincoln and Daniel Boone. Merle Oberon was the ravishing Eurasian born, British star transformed by producer Samuel Goldwyn into a slice of all-American womanhood (precursor of such later stars as Audrey Hepburn) whose beauty took one's breath away long enough to forget that her acting left only her breathless. The still itself looks very much as if it were a color transparency with its colors heightened by hand tinting.

SAMUEL GOLDWYN
presents

GARY
COOPER
MERLE
OBERON
in
THE
Cowboy
AND
the Lady

with
PATSY KELLY · WALTER BRENNAN
FUZZY KNIGHT · MABEL TODD
HENRY KOLKER
Directed by H. C. POTTER
ORIGINAL STORY BY LEO McCAREY and
FRANK R. ADAMS · SCREEN PLAY BY S N
BEHRMAN and SONYA LEVIEN
RELEASED THRU UNITED ARTISTS

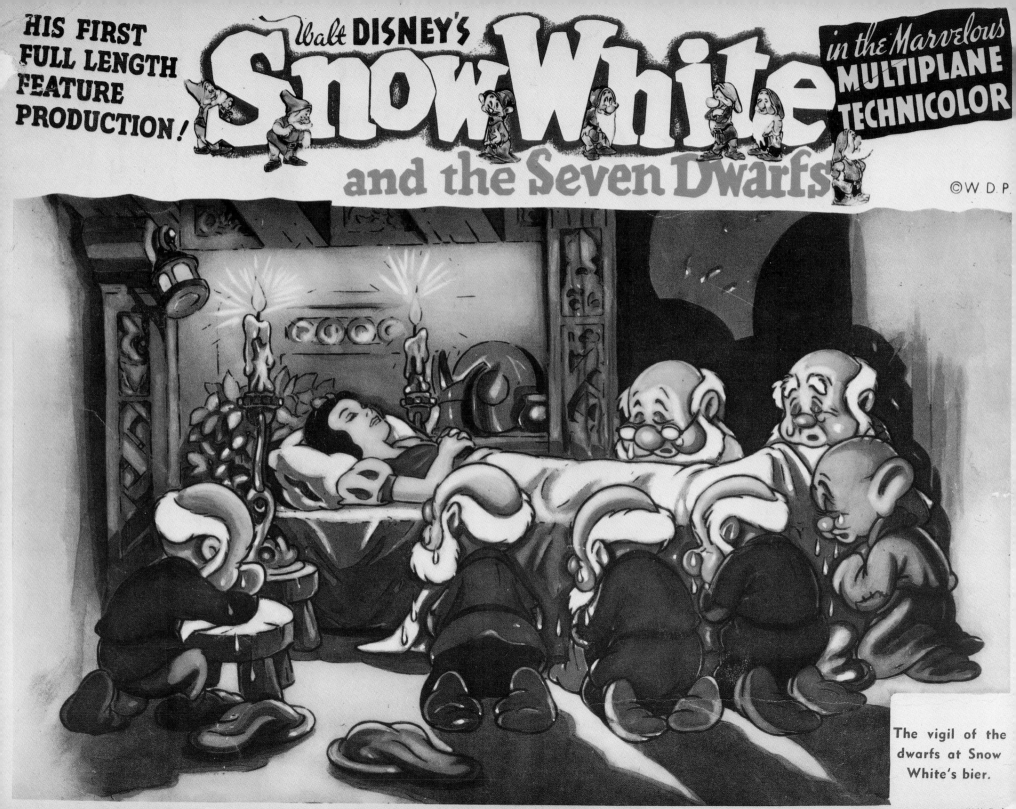

HIS FIRST FULL LENGTH FEATURE PRODUCTION!

Walt DISNEY'S Snow White and the Seven Dwarfs

in the Marvelous MULTIPLANE TECHNICOLOR

©W.D.P.

The vigil of the dwarfs at Snow White's bier.

COUNTRY OF ORIGIN U.S.A.

SNOW WHITE AND THE SEVEN DWARFS (RKO 1937) was Disney's and everyone else's first full-length feature animated production, and though it's easy to say so now, it has never been surpassed. Original Lobby Cards from the early Disney animated features are today among the most valued and highly priced of all movie artifacts.

HAVING A WONDERFUL TIME (RKO 1938). The holiday postcard home with the good healthy outdoors fun of horses and heroes and love, contrasting with the cramped subway city life of the working girl bothered by city slickers, illustrated here, is a brilliant 'come-on' stroke. The idea for this lobby advertising was inspired by old postcards.

DR EHRLICH'S MAGIC BULLET (WB 1940). Poor Dr Ehrlich, given short shrift in the film's title. It appears from this Lobby Card that Dr Ehrlich was the real-life scientist who invented the condom, here rocketing across the title card in this latest in Warner Brothers' successful mini-genre – the biographical picture – the series that gave the screen *Zola, Pasteur, Florence Nightingale (White Angel), Juarez*, etc. Ten years after playing *Little Caesar*, Edward G. Robinson was still the gangster Czar in the public's mind, and though his acting range far exceeded a talent for playing small time hoods, he was never allowed to forget his first and greatest success. This two-edged blessing necessitated special consideration in the selling of a subject as serious as this film. Thus, the speeding condom is made up to resemble the gangster's bullet, while at the same time a special message clearly states (though in much smaller type) that this is not a gangster picture. Of course, in 1940, they couldn't very well play up the fact that the deadliest enemy of all was . . . VD.

NOT A GANGSTER PICTURE BUT
. . . a war on the deadliest public enemy of all!
EDWARD G.
ROBINSON
DR. EHRLICH'S
MAGIC BULLET
WITH
RUTH GORDON · OTTO KRUGER · DONALD CRISP
Directed by WILLIAM DIETERLE • A WARNER BROS.-First National Picture
Original Screen Play by John Huston, Heinz Herald and Norman Burnside • From an idea by Norman Burnside • Music by Max Steiner
Presented by
WARNER BROS.
A
Country of Origin U. S. A.
THIS ADVERTISING MATERIAL IS THE PROPERTY OF VITAGRAPH, INC. AND IS LEASED PURSUANT TO AN AGREEMENT WHICH PROVIDES: "THE EXHIBITOR AGREES THAT THE ADVERTISING MATERIALS *** ARE LEASED FOR USE ONLY IN CONJUNCTION WITH THE EXHIBITION AT THE THEATRE SPECIFIED *** OF THE RESPECTIVE MOTION PICTURES IDENTIFIED IN SUCH MATERIALS AND ONLY FOR THE PURPOSE OF PROPERLY ADVERTISING AND EXPLOITING SAID RESPECTIVE MOTION PICTURES AT SAID THEATRES AND THE EXHIBITOR AGREES THAT HE WILL NOT TRADE, SUBLEASE, SELL, GIVE AWAY OR OTHERWISE USE OR PERMIT OTHERS TO USE SUCH MATERIALS."

DODGE CITY (WB 1939). By now, Technicolor was no longer a novelty. A film in Technicolor enhanced its prestige and box-office potential. This action-packed title card, short on design but high on octane and dramatic punch, hurls all of its appeal straight out at us: Errol Flynn's name is blazoned in banner headlines above the title, and by itself, even though both of his leading ladies (Ann Sheridan, who had just erupted as the last great sex star of the thirties, was the good-time gal who lost Flynn to de Havilland, his perfect mate) were already box-office stars in their own right. The punch ups, the shoot-outs, the on-rushing train, the galloping cowboys, the cattle drive, and the large cut-out parts of the stars, combine to give us a sense of immediacy and action on the large scale.

ERROL FLYNN
DODGE CITY
in TECHNICOLOR
OLIVIA de HAVILLAND · ANN SHERIDAN
ALAN HALE · FRANK McHUGH · BRUCE CABOT ·
Directed by MICHAEL CURTIZ
A WARNER BROS. PICTURE

DARK VICTORY (WB 1939). When she made this movie, Bette Davis was considered to be the premier actress, and replaced Shirley Temple as the biggest female box office draw in the country. On the screen Davis was a fighter. She had the comparable qualities of the popular male stars of her time yet never lost the audience's respect for her as a woman. She had the courage of her convictions, and to her submission was not defeat. *Dark Victory* was a typical sentimental woman's picture to which Bette Davis brought the stature of Greek tragedy. Humphrey Bogart (playing the third male lead after George Brent and along with Ronald Reagan) had up to and including this point in his career been little more than a reliable all-purpose supporting actor at the studio. With *The Maltese Falcon*, made a couple of years later, he was to move into Bette Davis' league. The yellow lettering against the orange flamed background gives the impression of the sun's life-affirming rays.

THE MALTESE FALCON (WB 1941) is John Huston's directorial debut; the story was by Dashiell Hammett. The stars were a collection of actors who'd long since given up thoughts of stardom. It launched Bogart on his career as a legend, Mary Astor went on to her Oscar, and everyone else connected with it was memorable. The cards from this film, not all memorable, are among the most valuable collectors' items.

CASABLANCA (WB 1942). A film with unlimited possibilities for exploitation becomes simply the means for the studio to present Humphrey Bogart, on his meteoric rise to the top, as a romantic star. What it really offered has been described, analyzed, chewed over non-stop, ever since. This perfectly ordinary card, showing two earnest people in a clinch, is worth several thousand dollars because of what we know about them, and the film.

HITLER'S CHILDREN (RKO 1943). These were the 'Hitler Youth', young Germans brainwashed into following the Fuehrer's call to a new, better and blonder Germany. No questions asked. Those foolish enough to try were tied up to a post and whipped, under the watchful eyes of their friends. Bonita Granville, who'd made a successful transition from being a child star (and is here being whipped) had sprung to fame as a poison-mouthed schoolgirl when she accused two of *These Three* (based on Lilliam Hellman's *Children's Hour*) of having a lesbian relationship. And for telling tales out of school they sure made her pay in *Hitler's Children*.

HITLER'S CHILDREN

BASED ON GREGOR ZIEMER'S SENSATIONAL BOOK "EDUCATION FOR DEATH"

YOU WERE NEVER LOVELIER (Col. 1942). To the world Ginger Rogers had been Astaire's ideal partner. She'd left him after one of the most rhapsodized partnerships in the annals of stage or film to pursue as great a success on her own. Astaire was alone. He had doubts about finding a suitable new partner, about holding on to the public's affection as a solo act as Ginger had. Opposite Paulette Goddard, Joan Leslie, and even the brilliant Eleanor Powell, he had done little more than tread water. He had begun to think of retiring. Then came Rita Hayworth. She was young; she was ravishing. She was the dream of every male in the country, and he was asked to co-star with her in her first film as star. He was nervous. She was tall, as well as young, and beautiful, and it seemed to him that she had no need of him. Instead he met a child-woman who offered him all she had. She looked upon him with the adoration the whole country had for this dancing idol, and which he now saw in her. *You Were Never Lovelier* was their second and last picture together. It was not a May-to-December romance, but a festival of love set to music, and Astaire was like a man (and artist) new born. Eleanor Powell was undoubtedly the greatest dancer he ever partnered, Cyd Charisse, the most classical, and Ginger, the sympatico of ham-on-eggs. But Rita was romance, and it gave him back the spark that has never left him.

Fred Astaire and Rita Hayworth—dancing and singing together!

FRED **ASTAIRE** ★ RITA **HAYWORTH**
in
"YOU WERE NEVER LOVELIER"
A COLUMBIA PICTURE

PRINTED IN U.S.A.

HOTEL FOR WOMEN (Fox 1939). 'The Petty Girl', the curvaceous ideal from the paintbox of George Petty, like the Vargas' Girl (Petty's successor at *Esquire* magazine, and rival in the pin-up calendar sweepstakes) were twentieth century versions of painters such as Kertcher whose nineteenth century 'pin-ups' were of nymphs and shepherdesses. Like Vargas', Petty's Girl had a smile for everyone. The difference between the styles lay in the slightly more pleasing ripeness of Petty's Girls. *Hotel For Women*, a Cosmopolitan production (film division of the Hearst publishing empire) employed Petty for this film. Over the years Vargas had been commissioned by the studios to design posters for films like *Flame of New Orleans* (Universal, see page 16), *Suddenly It's Spring* (Paulette Goddard, Paramount), *Du Barry Was A Lady* (Lucille Ball, MGM) and *Ladies They Talked About* (Barbara Stanwyck, WB). Clearly, *Hotel For Women* has no stars, but promises to be full of fun by offering similar daydreams in the shapes and faces of several upcoming young starlets, such as Linda Darnell, Lynn Bari, et al.

The nominal star, plumb columnist and party-giver Elsa Maxwell, whose fame rested on bringing rich fat men together with life's equivalent of the Petty Girl come-true, and then prattling about it, and them, in her columns, makes her film debut here. It was not uncommon for studios, especially 20th Century Fox, to hire widely syndicated columnists for one or two inexpensive films and in return to get the studio a lot of free space plugging their other films in the flattered columnist's columns. It was while making this film that the ravishing teenage brunette Linda Darnell met cameraman Peverell Marley, who made her look even better than Petty, and whom she married.

Elsa Maxwell's
HOTEL FOR WOMEN
Elsa says:
"Girls do depend on men (the dogs!)... some for excitement . . . some for fame... and some even for love!"
A 20TH CENTURY-FOX PICTURE
DARRYL F. ZANUCK IN CHARGE OF PRODUCTION
A Cosmopolitan Production
LINDA DARNELL
ELSA MAXWELL
KATHARINE ALDRIDGE
JUNE GALE
JAMES ELLISON
JOHN HALLIDAY
ALAN DINEHART
JOYCE COMPTON
ANN SOTHERN
LYNN BARI
JEAN ROGERS
AMANDA DUFF
DIRECTED BY GREGORY RATOFF
ASSOCIATE PRODUCER RAYMOND GRIFFITH
SCREEN PLAY BY KATHRYN SCOLA AND DARRELL WARE
BASED ON A STORY BY ELSA MAXWELL AND KATHRYN SCOLA
B

SULLIVAN'S TRAVELS (Par. 1941). Clearly, from the need to capitalize on the *Lake* image in the shape of a famous cartoon, here on the border of the card (but dominating the poster for this brilliant, wickedly funny social satire about Hollywood), the studio shows that it didn't know how to sell this film, written and directed by Preston Sturges. Literally overnight, the explosive little teenage blonde with the unruly hair had the year before shot to stardom in what had only been the second of two female supporting roles in the male dominated action film, *I Wanted Wings*. This still is one of the few restful, and untypical moments in the film, and tells us no more about what to expect than the illustration on the side – but in 1941 the twenty-year-old Constance Ockleman, fresh from her success in *I Married A Witch* and about to be teamed up with Alan Ladd to become one of the decade's most memorable film duos, was probably all that was needed to draw the public into the theatre.

CABIN IN THE SKY (MGM 1943). The Vernon Duke musical was adapted from the stage by Vincent Minelli (with additional songs by Harold Arlen) in his solo-directorial debut in what was an audacious novelty for a film of that time, an all-black cast. Audacious because an expensive musical could not expect to recoup its money from a black audience (see *Hallelujah!*, page 49), and there was little hope that enough of a white public existed for such a film. It was not until 1954 that *Carmen Jones* (the all-black musical based on the Bizet opera) broke through the color barrier to reach a popular audience. Though Ethel Waters was one of the great musical stars of her day, MGM had a vested interest in spotlighting young, beautiful Lena Horne, who at one point the studio had planned to pass off as Mexican and for whom they even created a special make-up, known as Egyptian Blend No. 5, to further lighten her already fair skin. But Miss Horne remained resolutely true to her own type, and the make-up was used instead to lend an 'exotic' tint to such 'white stars' as Hedy Lamarr and Ava Gardner. With *Cabin in the Sky*, as with *Hallelujah!*, the art is once again a very stylish tribute to its subject, as can be seen here in the work of New York theatrical cartoonist Al Hirschfeld – note the signature bottom right of the drawing. Each card, as well as the poster, had a different Hirschfeld drawing.

M-G-M's Happy Hit!

CABIN IN THE SKY

Brilliant cast of entertainers!

★ ETHEL WATERS
★ Eddie "ROCHESTER" Anderson
★ LENA HORNE
★ Louis Armstrong   ★ Rex Ingram
★ Duke Ellington & His Orchestra
★ The Hall Johnson Choir

A Metro-Goldwyn-Mayer PICTURE

WINTERTIME (Fox 1943). This is fine bit of schmerm art. It happens to be the last of dimpled Norwegian-born Olympic ice skating champion Sonja Henie's lush, but no longer sparkling, musical escapades for the studio. She had been the highest paid star in films. Her leading men – Tyrone Power, Don Ameche and John Payne – all tall, dark and very handsome, chosen to complement her small, blonde and fair appearance, had been the studio's top male stars. *Wintertime* co-starred two such male types, Cesar Romero and Cornel Wilde, though Romero would never be a star, and Wilde was yet to become one. Popular band leaders and their troupes were a frequently used addition to mindless escapist plotless musicals. Miss Henie had already appeared with the best known band in the land, Glenn Miller and his orchestra, when she didn't need him to help pull in an audience, and now when she did, she was given Woody Herman. She completed her contract with this film and was allowed to sink or swim on her own merits.

ZIEGFELD FOLLIES (MGM 1945, released 1946) was the last of the MGM series that used the name of the legendary showman as a lure to attract a public for whom the Ziegfeld name had taken on the status of Monte Carlo, Paris, Folies Bergère, and the Moulin Rouge, as an instant catch phrase to conjure up glamor, color, beautiful girls, music, comedy and escape. The film was a collection of comedy sketches and musical numbers, and was hardly the 'Greatest Production since the Birth of Motion Pictures', but it was a fun filled technicolor feast. Rather than feature one member of the all-star cast over any of the others, or crowd the poster and title card with all of their famous faces, the idea of this title card was to spotlight the essence of the Ziegfeld appeal. No matter how famous the stars in his revues, it was the girls, and their costumes (or lack of same), that was the talk of the town. Alberto Vargas (see *Hotel For Women*, page 145), the popular *Esquire* magazine pin-up illustrator, whose career began in the 1920s and whose drawings included a number of the most famous Follies' girls in their day, was a natural choice to illustrate this poster.

GREATEST PRODUCTION SINCE THE BIRTH OF MOTION PICTURES!
M·G·M's
Ziegfeld Follies
in Technicolor
FRED ASTAIRE
LUCILLE BALL
LUCILLE BREMER
FANNY BRICE
JUDY GARLAND
KATHRYN GRAYSON
LENA HORNE
GENE KELLY
JAMES MELTON
VICTOR MOORE
RED SKELTON
ESTHER WILLIAMS
and WILLIAM POWELL
with EDWARD ARNOLD · MARION BELL
BUNIN'S PUPPETS · CYD CHARISSE
HUME CRONYN · WILLIAM FRAWLEY
ROBERT LEWIS · VIRGINIA O'BRIEN
KEENAN WYNN
Directed by VINCENTE MINNELLI
Produced by ARTHUR FREED
A METRO-GOLDWYN-MAYER PICTURE
Copyright 1945 Loew's Incorporated
Country of Origin U.S.A.

THE GIRL FROM JONES BEACH (WB 1949). Virginia Mayo, the wholesome, cuddly Petty Girl come to life from out of the chorus of Samuel Goldwyn musicals, gained fame as one of the most popular glamorous musical and romantic comedy stars of Hollywood in its last decade as a major industry. Though she was paired with most of the top male stars of the time, James Cagney (twice), Alan Ladd (twice), Danny Kaye (four times), Burt Lancaster (twice) and Ronald Reagan (twice), she was never to make a memorable 'click' in the public's mind. At the peak of her popularity she was described by the then Sultan of Morocco as 'tangible proof for the existence of God'. Eddie Bracken, not pointing, is the man who didn't become President.

HOUSE OF WAX (WB 1953). 3-D was a gimmick. Unlike color (see *Becky Sharp*, page 103) or later, Cinemascope (see page 18) it was never taken seriously by the studios, and the first few films in the process relied almost totally on the novelty of stereoscopic images, reaching out at the public from the screen (a novelty which dated back to the stereo-scopic cards popular at the turn of the century). However, the eyestrain caused by the need to wear special colored glasses (one lens was green, the other red) limited 3-D's popularity, and by the time studios started to use it for their major productions in musicals – *Kiss Me Kate* (MGM) – and for star vehicles like Rita Hayworth in *Miss Sadie Thompson*, the vogue was over and the films were released in standard vision. But for a brief time it did give the art departments something to wrestle with, as they once had with sound. Here the direct shock of audience participation is conveyed by including an audience staring up at a screen, with the characters, or bits of the action, framed to suggest spine tingling, mind chilling horror, so real it can't be contained by the screen.

WARNER BROS. BRING YOU THE FIRST FEATURE PRODUCED BY A MAJOR STUDIO IN 3D!
NATURAL VISION
3 DIMENSION
COLOR BY
WARNERCOLOR
"HOUSE OF WAX"
STARRING VINCENT PRICE · FRANK LOVEJOY · PHYLLIS KIRK
COPYRIGHT 1953 WARNER BROS. PICTURES DISTRIBUTING CORPORATION. PERMISSION GRANTED FOR NEWSPAPER AND MAGAZINE REPRODUCTION. MADE IN U.S.A.
Property of National Screen Service Corp. Licensed for display only in connection with the exhibition of this picture at your theatre. Must be returned immediately thereafter.
53 \263

UNTAMED (Fox 1955). Susan Hayward and Tyrone Power were among the superstars of the decade. Together or alone, they were a powerful box office attraction. Cinemascope was still new. In the early nineteenth century the British artist Henry Aston Barker went outside the confines of the rectangular shaped canvas, to illustrate more than the normal eye could see at one time. In the late 1920s, cinematographers began to toy with the same idea, but it was not until 1953, when 20th Century Fox produced the biblical spectacle *The Robe*, that Cinemascope and other wide-screen processes became an integral part of the American film. The size of the screen, curving from one side of the theatre to the other, embraced the spectator and involved him in the action without the use of eye-boggling lenses. From the outset it was envisaged as a new process that would become a mainstay of the industry and help to bring the public back to the movie houses. The sound, projected from several speakers to give the illusion of direct talk, had a thrill of its own, while the image, with subjects specially selected for its horizontal appeal, had novelty (though too much of the screen was now taken up by people lying across it instead of standing up). Close-ups looked awkward and were not used. Cinemascope, still fresh from the triumphs of *The Robe* and the all-star comedy *How To Marry A Millionaire*, was thus given preferential billing in all ads and if this one doesn't say it, nothing does. Of course Cinemascope quickly became standardized, and though the screens were now larger, the attraction soon waned.

AFRICOLOSSAL!
in
CINEMASCOPE
20th CENTURY-FOX presents
UNTAMED
starring
TYRONE POWER
SUSAN HAYWARD
RICHARD EGAN
The most violent canvas of love and adventure ever filmed!
COLOR BY DE LUXE
Directed by
HENRY KING
with John Justin
Agnes Moorehead
Hope Emerson
Produced by
BERT E. FRIEDLOB and WILLIAM A. BACHER · Screen Play by TALBOT JENNINGS, FRANK FENTON and MICHAEL BLANKFORT
Adaptation by Talbot Jennings and William A. Bacher · From the Novel by Helga Moray
Copyright 1955 20th Century-Fox Film Corp.
COUNTRY OF ORIGIN U. S. A.
1
Property of National Screen Service Corp. Licensed for display only in connection with the exhibition of this picture at your theatre. Must be returned immediately thereafter.
55-54

Printed in Hong Kong